PLANNING
YOUR
ESSAY

D0498734

POCKET STUDY SKILLS

Series Editor: **Kate Williams,**
Oxford Brookes University, UK

For the time-pushed student, the *Pocket Study Skills* pack a lot of advice into a little book. Each guide focuses on a single crucial aspect of study giving you step-by-step guidance, handy tips and clear advice on how to approach the important areas which will continually be at the core of your study ethic.

Published

Blogs, Wikis, Podcasts and More   *Andy Pulman*
Brilliant Writing Tips for Students   *Julia Copus*
Getting Critical   *Kate Williams*
Planning Your Essay   *Janet Godwin*
Referencing and Understanding Plagiarism
   Kate Williams and Jude Carroll
Science Study Skills   *Sue Robbins*

Further titles are planned

Pocket Study Skills
Series Standing Order
ISBN 978-0230-21605-1
(outside North America only)

You can receive future titles in this series as they are published by placing a standing order. Please contact your bookseller or, in case of difficulty, write to us at the address below with your name and address, the title of the series and the ISBN quoted above.

Customer Services Department, Macmillan Distribution Ltd Houndmills, Basingstoke, Hampshire RG21 6XS England

POCKET STUDY SKILLS

Janet Godwin

PLANNING YOUR ESSAY

palgrave
macmillan

First published 2009 by
PALGRAVE MACMILLAN

Palgrave Macmillan in the UK is an imprint of Macmillan Publishers Limited, registered in England, company number 785998, of Houndmills, Basingstoke, Hampshire RG21 6XS.

Palgrave Macmillan in the US is a division of St Martin's Press LLC, 175 Fifth Avenue, New York, NY 10010.

Palgrave Macmillan is the global academic imprint of the above companies and has companies and representatives throughout the world.

Palgrave® and Macmillan® are registered trademarks in the United States, the United Kingdom, Europe and other countries

ISBN-13: 978-0-230-22067-6
ISBN-10: 0-230-22067-3

This book is printed on paper suitable for recycling and made from fully managed and sustained forest sources. Logging, pulping and manufacturing processes are expected to conform to the environmental regulations of the country of origin.

A catalogue record for this book is available from the British Library.

A catalog record is available from the Library of Congress.

10 9 8 7 6 5 4 3 2 1
18 17 16 15 14 13 12 11 10 09

Printed in China

Contents

Acknowledgements

I thank Kate Williams, colleague, series editor and friend for her unflagging enthusiasm and support; colleagues who allowed access to materials used; the many students I have supported over the years for having taught me as much as I have taught them (and in particular those who kindly contributed to this book); my daughter Sallie for her common sense and perceptive illustrations and my son Oli for his patience (and as he starts university this year I hope he reads this book!).

Introduction

It is one of the pleasures of working in a university study advice service to see students' marks improve as they begin to understand that there is a generic structure to writing essays. Students concentrate hard on finding facts and trying to 'write the right answer' when they are really being assessed on how they present their argument.

The guide is designed to be easy to follow and picks up the areas that most tutors say are issues for undergraduates at university. It aims to demystify the process of essay writing at university in a 'show not tell' fashion, and uses clear, concise text with illustrations, examples and tips included where this will clarify the point.

This 'quick reference guide' to essay writing covers the complete process: from planning the task, timeline and word count through analysing the question, structuring your essay, to the drafting and redrafting stages. Finally, there is advice about how to reference and use appendices, and then tips on how to use the feedback you get from your tutor. So try the book and see your marks rise!

How to use this guide

You can use this guide just to dip in and out of if you know what you are looking for. For example, you may have lots of ideas but find it hard to structure your essay. For this, go to Chapter 7, which suggests structures for different types of essay.

However, if you find the whole process of essay writing at university a bit daunting or your feedback has highlighted areas needing development, then start at the beginning and work your way through. You can skip bits you don't need for now, but as the guide is quite short why not just browse through it all?

Janet Godwin

The purpose of essays

Essays are set so you can display your knowledge and understanding. They may have different formats depending on your subject. If you have been given a format to follow make sure you follow it as closely as you can.

JUDGE

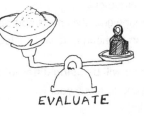

EVALUATE

How does doing an essay display your knowledge and understanding?

Writing the assignment involves you in different activities which improve your understanding of the topic.

To write an effective essay you must:

▶ have a clear idea of what you are being asked to do
▶ gather information
▶ present your argument
▶ use the language and style most appropriate to the discipline you are studying and
▶ do all of this in a limited time and limited word count.

In doing this you will be using different academic skills:

▶ decision making to focus your work
▶ research skills
▶ planning skills to produce a logical argument
▶ writing skills used in a way suitable to your discipline
▶ time management and ability to work to deadlines.

What does your tutor want?

Your tutor wants to see that you have:

- addressed any *learning or knowledge outcomes* either for your course or this particular piece of work (p. 23)
- followed course or field *professional standards and conventions*, for example a business report format or addressing ethical issues for social work
- taken a viewpoint and *developed an argument* to support this
- *evaluated the evidence* you have found – ask if it is relevant, up to date and from a reliable source (p. 87)
- *shown a clear link between theory and practice*, usually by providing examples such as linking educational theory to actual classroom situations, maybe from your own practice
- followed academic criteria, usually *by researching and using a range of reliable sources* and *referencing these correctly*
- shown *transferable skills* such as *time management* and *presentation* of your work, for instance using a computer.

LOOK at your learning outcomes

The assessment criteria are designed to test the learning outcomes, but what does the term 'learning outcomes' mean?

The learning outcomes are what you are supposed to know as a result of doing your course. It is up to you to **show** that you have learnt these and **can demonstrate** this by some method of assessment. Helpfully, these are usually outlined for you in your course handbook or given with your assignment.

Example question: *How well does provision meet mental health need?*

Learning outcomes that need to be demonstrated for this essay:

1 Ability to create an appropriate psychological profile for the chosen service user which demonstrates an understanding of evidence-informed practice in relation to the issues being presented.
2 Knowledge and application of ONE social work theory and/or method to the process of assessment and intervention related to the service user.

Most students do not use the learning outcomes effectively. If you learn to interpret these you can target exactly what your tutor wants in a piece of work. They are often written in difficult language so put them in your own words.

How students' and tutors' views of what is needed differ

It would be useful to know if students and tutors have different ideas about what is important in an essay. If you know what your tutors are looking for you can match their expectations to maximise marks.

Cover up the last two columns and put in order how important *you* think the different criteria are. Compare this with the results from Norton's (1990) research. If there are any surprises for you here, make a note of it now so you can check that your next essay matches with the tutors' view below.

Criteria	Your ranking	Tutors' ranking	Students' ranking
Answer the question		1	1
Understanding		2	4
Argument		3	7
Relevant information		4	3
Structure/organisation		5	6
Evaluation/own view		=6	8
Presentation/style		=6	9
Wide reading		8	5
English/spelling		9	10
Content/knowledge		Not ranked	2

Norton's (1990) students' vs. tutors' ranking of essay writing criteria

How do students' and tutors' criteria for a good essay vary?

According to Norton (1990) both students and tutors put *answering the question* as the most important criterion but students thought content and knowledge was the next most important thing. Tutors, however, thought *understanding* and *argument* were much more important than, say, wide reading. This shows a key difference between the student and tutor perspective: your tutor is less interested in you displaying knowledge; he or she knows that already. Your tutor **wants you to show your understanding by developing an argument using relevant information in a well-structured piece of work.** S/he is also interested in you having a view and being able to evaluate evidence.

Take a look at the criteria Norton produced and compare this with your own view, taking care to notice any differences. These will be the *key ways* you can focus on to improve your essay writing.

So this tells us you need to: Worry less about the content and more about **showing your understanding** and **arguing your own viewpoint.** Target this and you may need to do less reading overall.

Assessment criteria

You can see now that there are differences between students' and tutors' views of what needs to be in a good essay. This fact is important, since the biggest difference when studying at university is that **you have to work out how to follow the assessment criteria for yourself**. However long ago it was for you, teachers at school did a lot of this for pupils and assignments were designed so they exactly matched the assessment criteria. As long as the advice and instructions were followed you were almost guaranteed to get it right. You may also have been allowed to submit a first draft, about which the teacher made helpful suggestions.

University is different. You may have just an essay question and assessment criteria, with no opportunity to show your work to your tutor before the deadline (which you will find is usually an absolute deadline).

For example: *Evaluate the proposition that a global monoculture will destroy diversity and difference*. Just where do you start? What exactly is your tutor looking for? How will it be assessed? This is where your assessment criteria are vital. They will provide clues to follow and learning to interpret these will allow you to match your tutors' expectations.

Have a look at your list of assessment criteria. The wording may vary but usually these follow the same pattern so it is worth looking at now.

Looking at *your* assessment criteria

Look at your **assessment criteria** now. Tick the ones in the table you are being asked for. This gets easier to do as you become used to academic language. It is important you get in the habit of checking which criteria you need to follow for *each essay* you start.

Tick the assessment criteria needed for your essay (then read the small print for each tick)	✔ or ✗
Addressing the question: does the essay clearly answer the question set and focus on the title throughout the essay?	
Essay structure: is this clear, logical and well defined with an introduction, middle and conclusion? Does the conclusion draw together points made in the middle and 'mirror' the introduction?	
Showing understanding: is this consistently demonstrated in a logical, coherent and lucid way with evidence of wider reading?	
Developing an argument: is this presented by a well-reasoned and supported argument based on the available evidence?	
Critical thinking/critical evaluation: is material presented in a critical manner, which critiques concepts or methods used and shows an appreciation of alternative perspectives and any current controversies?	
Use of language and academic style: does it provide a well-presented, readable and generally clear essay which the reader wants to read, and does it show correct spelling and grammar use?	

Adapted from Elander et al. (2006)

Groundwork

Before you do ANYTHING else find out the details listed below. A small amount of time finding out these now will save you loads of time later on when you are up against the deadline. This is your **groundwork**.

What?	Why?
Deadline date, time and place to hand in	So you can plan stages of the essay to manage your time and workload effectively to *avoid an 'all-nighter' or last-minute panic.*
Word count or number of pages	This limits the amount of research done to what you can actually use. This *saves wasted effort.*
Format/structure	The tutor likes it done this way; s/he thought of it and if you follow this it *should address all the learning outcomes.* You would be mad to ignore this.
Percent worth	*This limits effort made to that required.*

Groundwork continued:

What?	Why?
Learning/knowledge outcomes	*So you can target these exactly*. Often these give you great starting points and suggest important areas you may have missed.
Professional outcomes	Many courses are designed to *train you* up in the *expectations of your future profession*.
Academic criteria (just look at the ones **for an A** for now).	So that you *demonstrate research done* (theory) and *apply this* (usually by linking to practice or examples). Also to show you can *use and acknowledge a range of views* and show where you found these by *referencing correctly*.

The stages of essay writing

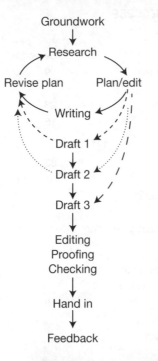

Groundwork

Research

Revise plan   Plan/edit

Writing

Draft 1

Draft 2

Draft 3

Editing
Proofing
Checking

Hand in

Feedback

What you need to know before you do ANYTHING!!!

Overview of the whole process

Groundwork

		See page
1	Find 'things you need to know'	9
2	Outline format (first plan)	
3	Select and analyse question	23
4	Do outline task timeline	15

Research

5 Do an information audit — 83
   a. What do I know?
   b. What do I need to find out?
6 Preliminary research
7 Further research (after Planning/Revising)

Planning

8 Outline format (see preparation above)
9 First plan (after preliminary research)
10 Adjust task timeline — 15
11 Revise plan after first draft
12 Revise plan after second draft

Writing

Editing, proofing and checking

Hand in

Feedback

What you need to know before you do ANYTHING!!!

Planning the whole process

You have a **set task** and a **limited amount of time** in which to complete it.

It is worth dividing up the time you have available to fit your time frame; adapt this to your particular strengths and build in time to cope with any difficulties you may have. The best way to do this is to do a **task timeline.**

You may be a good planner but find you always rush at the last minute because your work is way over word count. This happens because you do not limit the content of the essay to the word count available and so spend unnecessary time and effort weeding out the research you so painstakingly collected. Or you may be dyslexic, so the reading and research will take longer than for other students. A dyslexic student will have to target reading carefully and use strategies to decide when to read deeply or not, and then arrange for someone to look over their work to spot proofreading errors.

This means everyone's task timeline will be different – but it is worth doing one. It need not be beautifully presented and you should certainly not waste time making it so. A rough working one will be just as good.

Time and task line

Here is an example of a time and task line for an essay set 1 November and due in 27 November.

Time	Task	Completed
1st–4th Nov	Groundwork Things you need to know Word/page count division Do task timeline Analyse question	3rd Nov
2nd–7th Nov	Preliminary research	8th Nov
7th Nov	Plan	9th Nov
11th Nov	Revise plan/edit	-
7th–10th Nov	Research	12th Nov
10th–14th Nov	Write draft 1	15th Nov
14th–16th Nov	Revise plan/edit	16th Nov
16th–18th Nov	Further research	19th Nov
18th–20th Nov	Write draft 2	16th–21st Nov
20th Nov	Revise plan/edit	22nd Nov
20th–23rd Nov	Further research and draft 3 if needed	-
23rd–26th Nov	Edit	24th Nov
26th Nov	Proofread	25th Nov
26th Nov	Checking	26th Nov
27 Nov	Hand in	27th Nov

work backwards (alongside rows from 7th Nov to 23rd–26th Nov)

What kind of planner are you?

Which of these describes you best?

Whichever one you are, you could do with a few tips …

I don't plan, ever

Ever heard of the saying, 'Failing to prepare is preparing to fail'? You would not go for a job interview without dressing smartly and trying to think of some intelligent-sounding answers and questions to ask. Without any planning your work will wander around and not really go anywhere. This will confuse both yourself and your reader. Planning helps you work through every step of the process with some purpose to ensure you use *all* the information you have been given to present an argument that actually answers the question.

All I seem to do is plan and not actually start the work

Over-planning can waste lots of time. You keep starting plans and then changing them. Producing pretty lists of what to do and coloured timetables or whatever makes you feel you are being a good student because you are working hard. The problem is you are *not producing anything your tutor can actually assess.* Every stage of your planning should be moving you closer to the finished product – your essay. This is why you need to consider first doing a task line (see p. 15) so that you keep moving on to the next stage.

I do plan but I never stick to it

This usually results in you not answering the original question – perhaps by answering the question you would like to have been set. Good analysis of the question and looking at the marking criteria and learning outcomes will make you more confident in your plan. Your plan can, of course, be adapted as you go along. Any changes must be checked to make sure you can fulfil all the criteria, and then double-check you are still answering the question.

I keep changing my mind, so I can't plan

This often happens, and results from lack of confidence about what you have to do. After dividing up your word or page count, *focus only on the information you have from analysing the question, learning outcomes and marking criteria.* You may of course do a few outline plans as you work through your ideas, but should soon be able to see which one would be more interesting to do. If you are still in any doubt, choose the one you can find good evidence for.

Becoming a better planner really will save you lots of time and effort.

Planning your planning!

To keep on target your plan will have to develop throughout the essay writing process

- **Start off** by dividing your up *word count* and follow any *structure or format* you have been given.
- **Next**, progress your plan by *analysing the question* (see p. 23), and refer to *your learning and professional outcomes* and the *marking criteria* (see p. 8).
- **Next** you need to do an *information audit* (see p. 83) to work out what you already know and what you will need to research.
- **Now** you will be able to *start to structure your essay* (see p. 28 and Chapter 7). Don't worry about this changing later on; this is a normal part of the process.
- **Lastly**, remember you will be *reviewing your plan* after your *first and second draft*, so you do not have to have the final perfect plan ready now.

Dividing up the word count

Don't worry. This is very simple and won't involve any serious brainpower for now. We are simply going to look at some of the ingredients needed for the essay and set out a very basic plan.

Ingredients

Word count (or number of pages) allowed
Format or structure (if given)

Method

Take the word count and divide it up as follows:

10% for the **introduction**
80% for the **main body**
10% for the **conclusion**

So **for a 2000 word essay** you will have:

200 words for the **introduction** (knock off a nought to get 10%: 200Ø); and therefore **200 words** for the **conclusion**; leaving

2000 – 400 = **1600 words** for the **main body**.

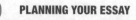

Dividing up the page count

If using pages do a similar calculation. Thus for 8 pages you would use a bit less than 1 page each for both the introduction and conclusion, leaving 6–7 pages for the main body.

So now your plan will look a bit like:

Introduction	10%	200 words
Main body	80%	1600 words
Conclusion	10%	200 words

Dividing up the main body

The next step is to divide up the main body. If you have been given any **format or structure** to work to you should look at it now. Headings or sections may already have been suggested. The best advice is to follow this format since it has been designed by your tutor to produce just what s/he wants to see in the essay. Alternatively, look at Chapter 7 for different types of essay and suggested structures for these to see if there is one you can use or adapt.

Your **word count** is **your budget** and you can use any variation that adds up to this for your main body, but *don't overspend* as that will use up valuable time (and effort) later 'making it fit' the word count.

Using our 2000 word example: we have **1600 words** to spend, so this may be:

    2 x 800   word sections   (divided into paragraphs)
    4 x 400   word sections
    5 x 300ish   word sections

The next step is to **analyse the question** (p. 23) and collect any **learning and professional outcomes** (p. 10) and **marking criteria** all together.

Analysing the question

In order to answer the question you first need to understand what you are being asked to do. There are **different types of words** in the title. A few easy steps deciphering these can help you work out all the clues in the question.

Helpful types of words in the question:

Word type	Example	Function
Process words (sometimes called the instruction, direction or keyword)	'Discuss', 'Evaluate', 'Critically analyse', 'Briefly outline'	Tells you the process you have to do; also indicates depth of research required.
Subject or **content** words	The main area under discussion.	Broad focus of answer (try to stick to this only).
Limiting or **scope** words	Dates, geographical area, number of examples.	Focuses the area to be examined; note this carefully.
Other **significant** words – key aspects	Any other aspects not covered above.	Pinpointing limit or scope of answer.

Adapted from Williams (1995)

Breaking down the question

Using highlighters or box and underlining as shown below identify the different words in the question.

Process or instruction word

Significant word (other propositions?)

Subject

Evaluate the proposition that a | *global monoculture*

will destroy diversity and difference

Key aspect (only destroy?)

Scope or limit of question

Assessment instruction (or process) words

These words tell you the **process** you have to do and indicate the depth of research needed. You will not need all of them – just make sure you understand the ones you are usually asked for.

Account for	Give reasons for.
Analyse	Break down into parts and examine, giving in-depth explanations. Show why these are important and how they relate or connect to each other.
Argue	Give the case for or against by acknowledging the case for and against, and using evidence to support your case.
Assess	Identify strengths and weaknesses. Make sure you come to a judgement.
Comment	Show you understand the topic, give your view, and provide evidence and examples.
Compare	Show similarities and differences.
Contrast	Show how subjects are different.
Critically analyse	See, analyse and add your reflections.
Critically evaluate	Weigh up the arguments for and against; assess the strengths, weaknesses and evidence for both sides. Support with models, approaches and/or theories.

Criticise	This is *not* about finding fault with a study or approach! Show that you can see the strengths and weaknesses of a view/theory and indicate where you stand. You must provide evidence, discuss this and draw a conclusion.
Define	Give clear, concise meanings. Show the limits of these.
Describe	Outline the main features. Keep it short; it is usually only the first part of a question.
Discuss	Identify significant features, show reasons for and against and the implications of these.
Distinguish	Show differences between.
Evaluate	Notice the word 'value' in 'evaluate'. Weigh up strengths and weaknesses and assess. Look at limitations, costs/benefits. Come to a judgement.
Examine	Look closely at, in detail.
Explain	Make clear and give details about how and why something is so. Give reasons.
How far/to what extent	Set out the arguments and evidence on both sides. Your conclusion will be somewhere between 'all' and 'nothing'. Be clear precisely where you are, and why you have reached that point.
Illustrate	Usually in a two-part question. Give examples and/or evidence to make your point clear.

Indicate	Point out, identify and clarify.
Interpret	Simplify; show what something might mean – especially data. Then make your own judgement.
Justify	Take a viewpoint and argue this, providing reasons and evidence.
Outline	Main features only; this is usually one part of a two-part question.
Prove	Establish that something is true with evidence and a clear argument.
Reflect	Examine an incident or experience. Look back at how you reacted, what went well or not so well, and what you would do differently in future.
Review	Examine critically, provide analysis and comment on important points.
State	Give brief, clear information. Do not give details or examples.
Summarise	Provide the main points in brief, in your own words
Trace	Show the sequence of how something happened or developed.

Analysing the structure

Think of your essay as parts of a puzzle that are linked but have independent roles to play.

This will prevent your introduction becoming the essay, make sure that the main body of your work flows, and allow you to draw a clear conclusion.

Making a diamond essay

Using a diamond structure will help you break the essay down into bite-sized pieces which will flow well when you put them all together. Here's how:

Imagine your whole essay as a ◇. It has:

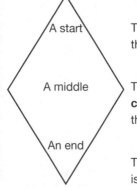

The **introduction** has its own structure and is **separate** from the **main body**.

The **main body** is the **development** of your **argument into clear sections** consisting of one or more paragraphs. Each of these paragraphs also has a start, middle and end.

The **conclusion** also has its own structure and purpose and is **separate** from the **main body**.

Thinking of your essay as a diamond will remind you that whatever *points you start, you have to finish off somehow*. This is the key to making your work flow.

A diamond essay – looking at the main body

Leave the introduction and conclusion for now and focus on the main body. This will be constructed of sections containing one or more paragraphs.

A **section** ◇ with one or more **paragraphs**

    will **link to** the **next section** ◇

        which **links to** the **next section** ◇

            ... and so on ... ◇

Until you get to the conclusion.

So all sections link together:

 link

       link

A diamond essay – paragraph planning

Each **paragraph** will also follow our **diamond pattern**: ◊

An opening sentence will be followed by supporting evidence and/or examples to back up your point. You may of course present an opposing argument as well, to show you are considering alternative viewpoints, but your motive here will be to show that your argument is best. This will be followed by a mini conclusion, which may be your comment or a link to the next section.

An opening or **'topic' sentence**,

followed by:

supporting evidence and/or **examples** to support or contrast with your point.

followed by:

A **mini conclusion** to the paragraph. Your **comment** or **link** to **next section**

Ask yourself: SO WHAT? (this will help you be analytical)

Essay diamond

The stages of essay writing are:

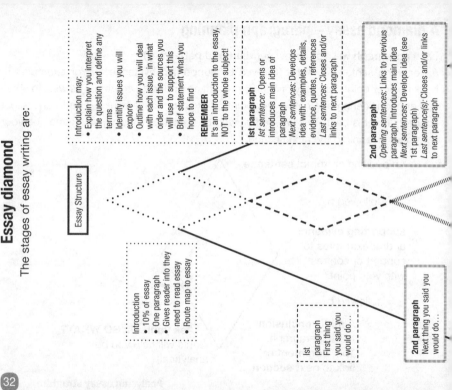

Essay Structure

Introduction may:
- Explain how you interpret the question and define any terms
- Identify issues you will explore
- Outline how you will deal with each issue, in what order and the sources you will use to support this
- Brief statement what you hope to find

REMEMBER
It's an introduction to the essay, NOT to the whole subject!

1st paragraph
1st sentence: Opens or introduces main idea of paragraph
Next sentences: Develops idea with: examples, details, evidence, quotes, references
Last sentences: Closes and/or links to next paragraph

2nd paragraph
Opening sentences: Links to previous 1st sentence. Introduces main idea
Next sentences: Develops idea (see 1st paragraph)
Last sentence(s): Closes and/or links to next paragraph

Introduction
- 10% of essay
- One paragraph
- Gives reader info they need to read essay
- Route map to essay

1st paragraph
First thing you said you would do…

2nd paragraph
Next thing you said you would do…

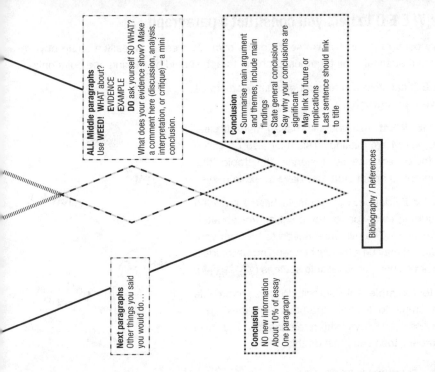

ALL Middle paragraphs
Use **WEED!** WHAT about?
EVIDENCE
EXAMPLE
DO ask yourself SO WHAT? Make a comment here (discussion, analysis, interpretation, or critique) – a mini conclusion.

What does your evidence show?

Conclusion
- Summarise main argument and themes, include main findings
- State general conclusion
- Say why your conclusions are significant
- May link to future or implications
- Last sentence should link to title

Next paragraphs
Other things you said you would do....

Conclusion
NO new information
About 10% of essay
One paragraph

Bibliography / References

Use W E E D to help you construct a paragraph

Every paragraph must make sense on its own. Your essay is really a string of paragraphs that should link together. Each paragraph should be making one point only.

W E E D can help you remember what needs to be in **every paragraph**.

W is for **What**. Ask yourself: have I made it clear what point I am making? This may also be called the topic sentence as it signals the 'topic' this paragraph is about. You may have to **explain** this.

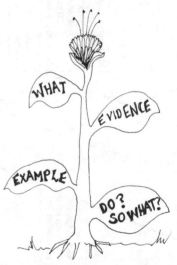

E is for **Evidence**. Ask yourself: have I provided supporting evidence for my point and/or an alternative view? The evidence needs to be from your reading. It may be a theory, concept, model or idea. Check you have used reliable sources (see p. 85).

E is for **Example**. Ask yourself: do I need to provide an example to illustrate the point I am making? If your essay title says 'with reference to …' **or** 'give examples' then you must do this.

D is for **Do**. Ask yourself: what do I do with the information given? If you ask yourself **'so what?'** then you should be able to see why your point is important. Explain this to your reader. This is the analytical bit that will get you those important extra marks.

Going deeper – the paragraph plan

Paragraphs are the building blocks of your essay. Use them properly and you are well on the way to constructing a good essay. **W E E D** will help you remember the basics of a paragraph. The **paragraph plan** below goes into more detail about how to make a good paragraph.

First sentence introduces the **point** that will be discussed in this paragraph. **Second sentence** explains or defines any **abstract, key or problematic terms**.

The **middle sentences** develop your point by providing:
     supporting evidence for your point   **(essential)**
     examples of this   (if needed)
     an **alternative viewpoint**   (maybe)

The final sentence(s) comments on the evidence given. **Ask yourself 'so what?'** Show why or how this is important; this **puts your voice** in the essay.
Conclude by giving any **consequences or implications of your argument** and **link** to the **next paragraph** as best you can. **Look back at the first sentence** of the paragraph to check you have **moved the argument on**.

Example of a good paragraph

In the example below, the highlighting corresponds to the four different parts of the paragraph.

What

It can also be argued, that in a country such as South Africa, which has gone through such a huge transformation, a dominant, powerful government is beneficial. As the ANC can afford to take a long term view over what changes and policies need to be implemented they can do this without worrying about how they are going to become elected again or adopting unrealistic, populist policies.

Example

Evidence

This view is shared by COSATU president Wille Mahida when he says, '… any threat to an ANC victory is a threat to political stability and the creation of legitimate political institutions' (Mail and Guardian 15.04.04, as cited in Southall and Daniel, 2005)*.

Do

This is especially important in newer democracies with a system of proportional representation as this can often create weak, inefficient coalition government which achieves little in countries which most need change.

*The student should have provided a page number as they used a direct quote

What makes this a good paragraph?

What   First sentence tells us the topic or point to be made in this paragraph.

Example   Explanation of why this is true.

Evidence   Evidence from a reliable source to support the point made; here you can use a newspaper as it has already been quoted in a reliable source.

Do   Final sentence links to first 'topic' sentence. This sentence effectively comments on and concludes this paragraph. It needs to link to the next paragraph as best you can.

Introductions and conclusions

Understanding introductions and conclusions

Introductions and conclusions are the most important parts of your essay. Do not skimp on these. They provide the framework for your work and tell your reader what to expect, what you found out and the relevance of your findings.

Think of them as the bedposts of your essay.

Even if the middle section of your essay is not perfect (a bit lumpy perhaps) a good introduction and conclusion will provide the impression of a well-constructed essay.

What is the purpose of the introduction?

Remember, your introduction is an introduction to the essay only, not the whole topic.

Your essay introduction has three functions:

▶ to catch your reader's interest
▶ to provide your reader with any information they need to understand your work
▶ to tell your reader what you intend to cover and how you will do this.

Writing your introduction – aspects to include

An effective introduction will have **three aspects** to it. It needs to provide your reader with:

Aspect 1: Any information needed to understand your work. This could be: how you interpret the question, setting the scene with a brief background, and any definitions of terms that need explanation from the title.

Aspect 2: A route map to your essay. This explains what you are going to do and how you are going to do it.

Aspect 3: Say what you will argue. This is optional. You may not want to give the game away at the beginning, but it is quite a good idea for you and your reader to be clear about your viewpoint. This is sometimes called the thesis statement.

So, producing a perfect introduction is as easy as:

  1 Information   **2** Route map   **(3?)** This essay will argue …

Aspect 1: Information your reader needs to know

The introduction is the place to make sure your reader has all the tools they need to understand your work.

How you interpret the question

Just supposing you interpret the question slightly differently to your tutor? If you explain what you understand of the question to start with, at least s/he will know your starting point.

Unless you make a serious error here this should not matter too much as long as you argue your case clearly.

Setting the scene with a brief background

This helps the reader to know what you consider the background to be and why this question needs to be addressed. Keep it brief, though. If you need to do a detailed background this should become a section of the essay itself.

Definitions of terms in the title

Define any specialist or complicated words in the title. Again, this clarifies where you are coming from and going to.

Aspect 2: What you are going to do and how this will be done

Tell your reader exactly what you are going to do and how you will do it. This gives your reader an idea of what to expect and shows you have a clear purpose. It also helps you to keep on track and work towards your conclusion.

Think of this as the *route map* to your essay:

What issues will you explore
in order to reach
your CONCLUSION
and exactly how will you do this.

Remember: Everything in your essay should be working towards your conclusion. This does not mean you will not show the opposing view; only that when you do this your viewpoint should be the stronger argument.

Aspect 3: Say what you are going to argue

Of course, you do not *have* to do this. But if you do, your tutors will know **where you are going with your argument** and can focus on how you get there. They may appreciate not having to figure this out by themselves by rewarding you with a better mark.

Remember: your tutor wants to see an argument and this will make it clear that he or she is getting one. It helps you clarify your own position and decide what your viewpoint really is.

What do I think?

And finally … a top tip about introductions

This may seem topsy-turvy but it is often better if you …

Write your introduction AFTER you have FINISHED the essay!

Why? Because as long as you know roughly what issues you are going to cover and how you will do this you will only have to rewrite the introduction *to fit the essay* you *actually wrote*. This tip also stops that old problem of your introduction becoming the essay itself because you fell into too much detail, too soon.

So … Although the introduction is part of the essay it is useful to think of it as a separate section, with its own structure and purpose.

Has this student produced a good introduction?

Below is an example of a student's introduction to an essay with the title: *Can environmental problems be solved within the current structure of the global political economy?*

Take a look at the writing, compare it with what you know makes a good introduction and see if you agree with the comments. The highlighting corresponds to the different aspects of the introduction.

Aspect 1

The global economy can be caricatured as a wolf in sheep's clothing; a docile outer image concealing a ravenous predatory instinct. Our 'shepherding' of the global economy is increasingly called into question as the threats posed by untold environmental change become ever clearer. Debate surrounding the relationship between environmental degradation and global economic activity is divided between powerful advocates of the status quo, and those who believe that we must urgently intervene to curb environmentally damaging practices. This essay will argue that it is not possible to solve global environmental problems within the current

Aspect 3

structure of the global political economy because the principles which underpin the free competitive free market unavoidably exploit it.

Analysis of student's introduction

> Visual image, a good attention grabber.

Aspect 1   **Information reader needs.** Good background, makes it clear there are two viewpoints.

Aspect 2   **Route map of the essay.** There is NO outline of the issues to be covered or how this will be done.

Aspect 3   **Say what you will argue.** The writer's position is clear, but it would be good to know what principles are being referred to here.

Did the student write a good introduction?

The student did write a good introduction, but it could be slightly improved.

It is a good introduction because:

▸ It got the reader interested in the first sentence.
▸ It provided the information and background the reader needed to understand the context (**Aspect 1,** see p. 41).
▸ The writer has clearly stated what they will be arguing (**Aspect 3,** see p. 43).

It could be improved by:

▸ Although the writer's position (**Aspect 3,** (see p. 43) is clear we don't know exactly what issues will be explored and how this will be tackled. Giving a route map or guide of exactly what will be covered in the essay and saying how this is going to be tackled would have solved this (**Aspect 2,** see p. 42). For instance, the writer may have used a company case study to illustrate the essay, or may have set some limit on the scope of the essay by examining one particular environmental issue. The introduction is the place to make this clear.

Writing the conclusion: its purpose

What is the purpose of the conclusion?

Your conclusion has four functions:

1 To present your main findings.
2 To provide your reader with *your conclusion* from this evidence.
3 To explain any implications of your conclusion for the future.
4 To answer the question – do this in the last sentence to give your reader a sense of satisfaction.

Writing the conclusion: aspects to include

The conclusion must tie everything up for your reader and give them a sense of satisfaction that the question has been answered. An **effective conclusion** needs to provide your reader with these **five aspects**:

Aspect 1: A recap of what the essay explores (one sentence if possible).

Aspect 2: A summary of your main findings. Your tutor does not want to wade back through your essay to sift for what you found out. So, do the work for them by presenting an overview of the main take-away points.

Aspect 3: A clear conclusion. Now you must present *your conclusion* from the evidence you provided. Your tutor may have a different opinion to you, so check your *evidence* really does *support your conclusion*.

Aspect 4: The implications of your conclusion. Looking to the future here shows your tutor not only that can you argue your way to a conclusion but that you can also relate this in practice. Show how your conclusion(s) impact, influence or are important in practice.

Aspect 5: Answer the question! Make the last sentence link directly to the title or question; this creates a sense of satisfaction for your reader.

What NOT to do in the conclusion

There are two things to be aware of about conclusions:

    1 No new information   2 Your evidence must support your conclusion

Example of unsupported statement in conclusion:

'Our world is heavily overpopulated ...'. The student put this in the main text with no supporting evidence and repeated it the conclusion; this earned the rebuke 'prove it' from the tutor.

If you come to a **conclusion that is not supported by your evidence** or is simply not in your essay *you are in big trouble*. It is OK if you ended up somewhere else – but you must show *how* you got there.

Do not put *any* new information in the conclusion: This is because you cannot provide the supporting evidence for it in the conclusion.

Tutors are not always concerned about the right answer but they *are* really **interested in your ability to take a view and argue your way towards your conclusion.** They also want to see that you have used respected evidence and examples (see p. 85), referenced these correctly (see p. 99) and used an appropriate academic style (see p. 88).

And finally … a top tip about conclusions

This may seem topsy-turvy but it is a good idea to:

Write a draft conclusion BEFORE you start the essay!

Why? Because it is much easier to argue your way through the essay if you have a rough idea of where you are going. You would not set out on a long journey without a destination (and hopefully a map: your plan in the case of an essay.) Of course you may not know what your conclusion is when you start, but as soon as you have an idea about this jot it down. Doing this will help you focus throughout the essay and also enables you to spot when you are wandering off the point.

Remember: everything in the essay should **support your conclusion**. You can **present alternative viewpoints** to show your argument is best and critique the evidence to **support your argument**.

Has this student produced a good conclusion?

Below is an example of a student's conclusion to an essay with the title: *Is the ANC's dominance in the post-apartheid era detrimental to democracy in South Africa?*

Take a look at the writing below, compare it with what you know makes a good conclusion and see if you agree with the comments. The highlighting corresponds to the different aspects of the conclusion.

Aspect 5
Answered the Q

Aspect 3
Clear conclusion

To conclude, it can be argued that ANC dominance is in many ways detrimental to democracy but it should be remembered South Africa has already made a dramatic change in terms of democracy. The ANC has managed to implement a thriving democracy in a volatile county, a difficult accomplishment. It was always going to be problematic to establish democracy in a country which had been without one for so many years. However, in theory at least, South Africans now live in one.

Aspect 2
Sum up main points

Aspect 4
Future implications

The ANC cannot be blamed for the lack of opposition parties and therefore a lack of real opposition to their rule. They have adopted measures to attempt to bring members of other parties into the cabinet. Nevertheless, it is hard to see a situation in the foreseeable future where the ANC will not be in government as the electorate in South Africa vote according to racial affiliations. As black South Africans make up the majority of the population, it appears likely that the ANC will remain in power. Unless black South Africans grow so increasingly disillusioned with the ANC that they turn to other political parties the dominance of the ANC looks unlikely to change. However, the future could hold a split amongst the left- and right-wing members of the ANC and thus could bring about a change to the ANC's dominance of South African politics.

Did the student write a good conclusion?

The student did write a good conclusion, but it could be slightly improved.

It is a good conclusion because:
- It answered the question (yes, but …).
- It came to a conclusion (ANC implementing democracy).
- It gave a summary of the findings in the essay.
- It looked to the future and some of the implications (ANC unlikely to change unless a split …).

It could be improved by:
- recapping briefly what the essay covered
- checking that the conclusion 'mirrors' the introduction: that is, it matches what you said you would do in the introduction.

Notice that it *did not matter* that the student **didn't put all the aspects in the order on p. 49** ; just that they were all there. It is a good idea to say what **the essay explored** at the **beginning of your conclusion**.

Introductions and conclusions checklist

Does your introduction ...	Yes	No
use words and phrases from the title?		
indicate the main areas of your discussion?		
show you know what issues these areas imply?		
make it clear what you did and didn't cover – useful if you need to limit the scope of the essay. Give reasons for your decision.		
make sure everything is linked to the question?		
say what you will argue or state your position (optional)?		
follow the introduction 1, 2, 3(?) (see p. 40)?		
Does your conclusion ...	**Yes**	**No**
recap what you looked at (one sentence)?		
summarise your main findings?		
state a clear conclusion that follows from the evidence in the essay?		
outline any implications of your conclusion – look to the future here?		
contain new ideas? (Unless they are implications or ideas for future research: no new information in a conclusion, please.)		
mirror your introduction? Look at the introduction and conclusion side by side: do they fit together? Did you do what you said you would do?		
answer the question directly – possibly in the last sentence?		

Adapted from Williams (1995).

What TYPE of essay are you doing?

Check your essay title for clues here. See if you can match up what you are being asked to do with the essay types below:

Argue	Discuss, Judge, Evaluate, Advocate, Analyse. Includes 'To what extent …' essays where you must finish by stating clearly the extent to which you think something is true or happened.
Inform	Describe, Review.
Compare/contrast	Identify two or more areas and show where they are similar and where they are different.
Reflect	Examine an incident/experience, and analyse how you reacted to inform your future practice and professional development.
Cause and effect	Examine why something happened (the cause) and the result (effect).

Planning an argument essay

In an argumentative essay you will be expected to take a viewpoint. You will have to identify points for and against your viewpoint and argue your way towards proving that yours is the more valid argument.

To start, jot down:

My **argument will be** that …

Points *for* this	Evidence and examples
1	
2	
3	
Points *against* this	Evidence and examples
1	
2	
3	
Discussion	Strengths of my argument
	Weakness of my argument
	Weakness of other argument(s)
	Strengths of other argument(s)

Planning a 'to what extent' essay

This is essentially an argument essay, but in your conclusion you will have to make a judgement on how much or how far you agree or disagree with something. As with an argument essay, you are expected to take a viewpoint and identify points for and against this.

Start by working out just how far you agree or disagree with the proposition in your question by using a continuum line.

Example question: *To what extent can we explain the persuasive role of advertisements in terms of the Elaboration Likelihood Model?*

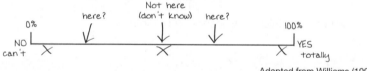

Adapted from Williams (1995)

This is your conclusion, so work yourself there using the structure given for an argument essay. Make sure it *is* clear to what extent you agree/disagree with the statement in the question: to some extent, to a large extent, not at all, yes completely or anywhere in between.

Planning an informative essay

For this type of essay you will be expected to present facts or information. You may be asked to describe or review something. An informative essay should be written in direct language and should present material in an orderly way. You may need to evaluate which aspects are most significant and you will need to have data to support, clarify and give authority to your work. As always, you should only use reliable sources (see p. 85).

You will also need to **decide how you will organise your material**.

Ideas include:

- Divide into topics, themes or issues; deal with them in order of importance.
- Start with the broad or general picture, then become more specific or detailed.
- Be chronological: present information in the order it happened.
- Conclude by identifying the most significant aspects and look ahead to any implications these may have for the future.

Planning a compare and contrast essay

In a compare and contrast essay you will be expected to identify themes that are similar or different and explain the importance of these. Try using a Venn diagram (shown below) as a thinking and planning tool. Put differences in the outer circles and similarities in the middle where the circles overlap.

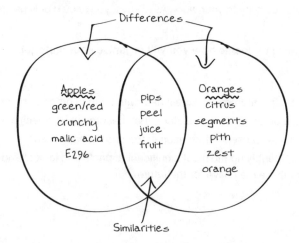

SCORE (2006)

Structure of a compare and contrast essay

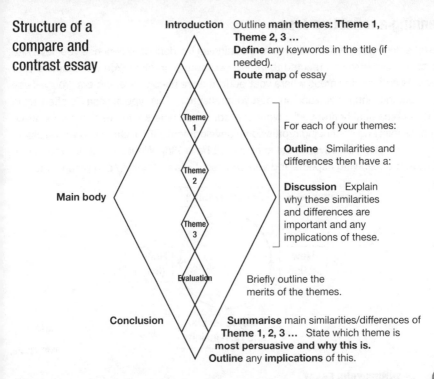

Introduction Outline **main themes: Theme 1, Theme 2, 3 ...**
Define any keywords in the title (if needed).
Route map of essay

Main body

Theme 1

Theme 2

Theme 3

For each of your themes:

Outline Similarities and differences then have a:

Discussion Explain why these similarities and differences are important and any implications of these.

Evaluation

Briefly outline the merits of the themes.

Conclusion **Summarise** main similarities/differences of **Theme 1, 2, 3 ...** State which theme is **most persuasive and why this is.** Outline any **implications** of this.

Planning a reflective essay

The reflective essay will expect you to examine an incident or experience you have had and to analyse how you reacted to inform your future practice. You will examine your strengths and identify areas where your performance needs development. You will use your reading to inform you and support your reflection. This type of essay is often set in fields such as healthcare, social work and education where you need to demonstrate competences and continuing professional development (CPD). Often you will be asked to use a specific reflective model such as Gibbs (1988). Whatever model you use, it will have the following aspects and you can use this as a thinking and planning tool.

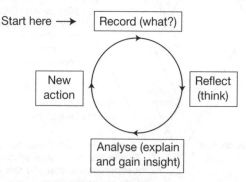

Start here ⟶ Record (what?)

New action

Reflect (think)

Analyse (explain and gain insight)

RMIT (2006)

Using a reflective model will help you analyse, reflect and develop an action plan for the future. In this type of essay the use of first person (I, my) is acceptable. You must relate your experience/practice to the literature available in the subject area.

The reflective essay is designed for you to use your experience and analyse this. You may have to challenge your beliefs, values, attitude and actions. You need to demonstrate why the experience/incident had a significant impact on your personal and professional learning and present an **action plan** to achieve this. If you have to include an action plan, **SMART** objectives can be useful.

Objective	How do I show this in my work?
S = Specific objective	Use precise wording.
M = Measurable	Say how you will evaluate/or measure your success.
A = Achievable	Outline the resources and support you will require to make your action plan work.
R = Relevant/realistic	Say why/how the objective is important to your goal(s).
T = Timescale	Give an idea of how long all this will take.

Adapted from Bournemouth University (2006)

Structure of a reflective essay

Introduction

Outline why **reflection is important** to your field …

Define any **keywords** in the title (if needed).

Route map of essay – identify the incident/experience, state any reflective model you will use to analyse this and say how your action plan will be presented.

Main body

Outline the incident, be objective and briefly explain any reflective model you are using.

Next you can *either*:

▶ use the steps in the reflective model

or

▶ use the stages of the incident and fit the model in as you go.

Remember: in both cases **link your reading in**.

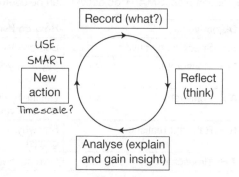

RMIT (2006a)

Conclusion

Summarise the main points that arose from your essay and **identify areas** you **need to develop in future**.

Present an action plan to show how you would tackle the situation next time; this shows what you have learnt. The action plan may have a timescale and use **SMART** objectives. Refer to, and follow, any guidance given.

Planning a cause and effect essay

In a cause and effect essay you will be expected to say why something happened (the cause) and what the result of this was (the effect). If there are a lot of possible causes and effects you may have to limit yourself to a few main ones. This is fine as long as you make it clear in your introduction which ones you are leaving out (or, if shorter, the ones you are including). Check your essay title and any learning outcomes – you have to ensure you are not missing out an important cause/effect.

If you are finding it hard to decide which ones to include, go for the most recent or most direct causes and effects. Decide if you are aiming simply to inform or whether you need to persuade your reader, as this will affect the language you use. After providing evidence and examples of causes and the effect(s) it is a good idea to finish by showing what could be done differently – a call for action – but keep a professional tone with this and don't lose your cool.

▸ If there are **multiple causes** you can deal with them one at a time: cause 1, then cause 2, then cause 3.
▸ For a **single cause** with multiple effects use a new paragraph for each effect.
▸ For a **chain reaction** (or domino effect) it is best to follow the order of events, so use a chronological (time) framework.

Structure of a cause and effect essay

Introduction

Identify the main causes and effects you will cover using the words 'cause' and 'effect'.

Define any **keywords** in the title (if needed).

Provide a '**route map**' of the essay. It should be clear whether you are writing to **inform** or **persuade**.

Main body: This may be ordered in *one* of the following ways:

Chronological – when the events occurred; or

Order of importance – most/least or vice versa; or

Themes – dividing the topic into parts or categories

Try using a grid to sort your ideas out.

The cause: why something happened	The effect: the result of this	Conclusion: is this an important cause?	What next: a call for action?

Conclusion

Summarise the main causes and the effects of these. State **which cause** you think is most important and **why** (use evidence from the essay). Do you have a **call for action** to make? Keep your cool!

Are exam essays different?

Yes, exam essays are different. You are working to a strict timescale and will only have access to what you can remember, unless it is an open book exam. Nevertheless much of the process is the same as writing a coursework essay. Try the following procedure.

Before the exam

Check the exam format so you can divide your time up. Find out:

▶ How long will the exam be? Do you have any reading time?

▶ How many questions will you have to answer?

▶ Are there any limits? For example: Answer one question from Section A and four from Section B.

▶ Are marks allocated to questions? If so, use this to divide up your time.

Section A and B = 50% each.
Exam 2½ hours = 150 minutes
150 - 30 mins for reading,
planning and proofreading - 120 mins
120/2 = 60 mins <u>each</u> for Section A and B.
Section A = 60 mins for 1 essay question
Section B = 60/4 so 15 mins per question (12½ % each)

In the exam

You will write a much better, more coherent answer if you devote a few minutes at the start of the exam to planning your time, analysing the question and doing a quick plan. This will prevent you from wasting time and possible marks by just writing down anything you can remember on the subject and expecting the poor marker sift out any relevant information.

Step 1: Plan your time

Quickly check that the exam format has not changed from your expectation. Recalculate your timings if it has changed; double-check this.

Exam only 2hrs = 120 mins - 20 mins (reading, planning
and proofreading) = 100 mins
100/2 = 50 mins each section
Section A = 50 mins for 1 essay question
Section B = 50/4 = 12 mins for each question (12½% each)

Step 2: Analyse the question (also see p. 23–4)

- Identify the process or instruction word (*discuss, outline, critically analyse*)
- What is the main subject or content?
- Are there any limits in the question?
- Any other aspects

Discuss the factors that a team need to consider
when designing a health promotion programme.

Step 3: Do a two-minute plan

Really, this will help: spend two minutes jotting down anything you think is relevant. Now go back to the question – is there anything you missed? Carefully check the instruction word; this tells you the detail to go into. Are there two parts to the question? Mind-map, bullet point or just scribble, but do it! Reread the question once you have done this; make any adjustments necessary and then try to put your points in order. Just write a number beside each and cross out anything you won't have time to do. Now you have your plan.

<u>Intro</u> - 5 mins
- Why health prog important
- Identify factors

<u>Middle</u> - 40 mins
Factor 1. ⎤ Outline each
Factor 2. ⎟ and how affects
Factor 3. ⎦ prog design

<u>Conclusion</u> - 5 mins
- Main points and implications for prog design

Whatever else you do, **stick to your time and plan**. If you are running out of time, make a few bullet points about what you would have mentioned, leave space in case you get time to return to the question later, and move on to the next question.

Turning your plan into an essay

Very briefly, you will probably be doing the following:

Quick introduction: be careful – don't let this become the essay
- Brief background of why the subject is important.
- Brief outline of what you will discuss.
- Definitions.

5 to 6 paragraphs: one for each point from the plan you are making. Follow the **paragraph plan** (p. 35) or use **WEED** from the essay diamond (**W**hat, **E**vidence, **E**xample and **D**o? see p. 34) for an easy way to remember what to put in a paragraph.

Conclusion:
- Sum up main points (probably one from each paragraph).
- State your overall conclusion; finish with any implications or action points of your conclusion – ideally you are looking to the future here.

Next question: Plan and produce your answer using the same process.

Allow 10 minutes at the end of the exam **to proofread**.

After the exam

Firstly, forget it for now. It is over: go off and celebrate or commiserate as appropriate!

When you get the result

Hopefully it will be good, or at least good enough, but you can learn a lot by reflecting honestly now on the experience whilst it is still fresh in your memory. Did any of the following happen?

- Ran out of time.
- Answered the question you wanted to see, not the one actually asked.
- Misread instructions.
- Did the wrong number of questions.
- Spent a ridiculous amount of time on one question so didn't do justice to the others.

For my next exam I will …

Using the list on the previous page, note down **what actually happened**.

Spent too long on Section A question (1 hr 15 mins) so only did three
questions from Section B & not the four I should have done.

Take a minute to think **what you are going to do** about this for next time.

I will … work out time for each question and stick to it. Use bullet points
& leave a space to return to if time. MOVE on to NEXT question on time …

Remember: Everyone makes mistakes. What is important now is that you learn from
your experience, so that you can improve for next time. That way at least you can
benefit from previous errors. If you don't reflect on what went well and what did not,
you are very likely to repeat the mistake. So be positive here and improve your grades.

9 Researching

Getting started is hard to do …

You will probably put this off for a while; after all, you have loads of time to do the essay. Then the moment of truth comes: the essay is due in soon and you have it all to do!

Look back to your **timeline** (p. 15). How much time do you really have? Do the groundwork (**collect all the information you need together,** p. 9), **dividing up your word count** (p. 20) and **analysing your question** (p. 23) as early as you can to break this cycle.

The next step is to get your **first thoughts** down and you can do this any way you like. The idea of this is just to put down anything you know about the subject, as quickly as you can. It gets you over the 'blank page' stage that can be paralysing. Try it out using the following steps:

1 Just get it down (anyhow – see opposite).
2 Add in any gaps in your knowledge or questions you have.
3 Cross out anything you think is not relevant.
4 Colour-code similar themes (just circle them for now).

First thoughts: ways to get them down on paper

BRAINSTORMING

FREE WRITING

MIND MAPPING

EXPLAINING TO A FRIEND

Still stuck?

Try answering these questions:

Who … Where …
Why … What …
When …

Or talking it though: with a friend, record your thoughts, tell the cat!

If you don't like using paper and pen, try using the computer. Mind-mapping programs such as MindManager or Inspiration may help.

What is the advantage of using mind-mapping software?

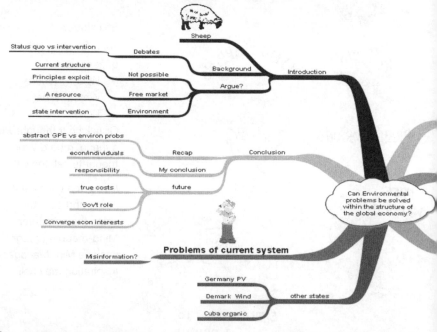

Programs such as Inspiration and MindManager allow you to plan visually using a variety of colours, shapes and word art or graphics from a picture library or the internet to produce a mind map. The example here uses Inspiration.

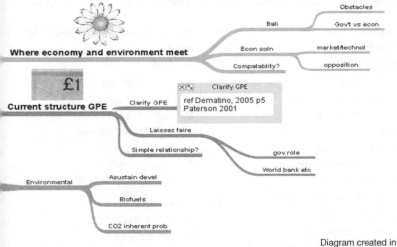

Diagram created in Inspiration ®
by Inspiration Software ®, Inc.

Converting your mind map to a linear outline

Perhaps the MOST useful function of mind-mapping software is its ability to transform your mind map into a list of headings with any notes and web links you have added – see the following example.

Can environmental problems be solved within the structure of the global economy?

I. Introduction
   A. Sheep
   B. Background
     1. Debates
      a. Status quo vs. intervention
   C. Argue?
     1. Not possible
      a. Current structure
     2. Free market
      a. Principles exploit
     3. Environment
      a. A resource
      b. State intervention

II. Where economy and environment meet
   A. Bali
     1. Obstacles
     2. Gov't vs. econ
   B. Econ soln
     1. Market/technol
     2. Opposition
   C. Compatibility?
     Clarify current GPE structure

III. Environmental
   A. A sustain devel
   B. Biofuels
   C. CO_2 inherent prob

IV. Current structure GPE
   A. Clarify GPE
      ref Dematino, 2005 p5
      Paterson 2001
   B. Laissez faire
      1. Gov role
      2. World bank etc
   C. Simple relationship?

V. Other states
   A. Germany PV
   B. Demark Wind
   C. Cuba organic

VI. Problems of current system
   A. Misinformation?

VII. Conclusion
   A. Recap
      1. Abstract GPE vs. environ probs
   B. My conclusion
      1. Econ/individuals
   C. Future
      1. Responsibility
      2. True costs
      3. Gov't role
      4. Converge econ interests

Diagram created in Inspiration ®
by Inspiration Software ®, Inc.

Converting mind map and outline to a document for editing

Finally, you can then convert your **mind map**, with the **outline of headings**, notes and web links you created into a **Word document**. This Word document will contain your mind map (as a picture) with the outline *that you can then edit*. Just select the mind map picture and delete it before you hand the work in.

You get a 30-day free download of the latest version of Inspiration from www.inspiration.com. MindManager is available as a 21-day free download from www.vtsdirect.com/index.html. These programs are the most widely used in education.

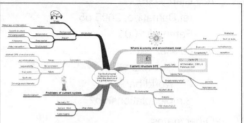

Can Environmental problems be solved within the structure of the global economy?

I. **Introduction**
  A. **Sheep**
  B. **Background**
    1. **Debates**
      a. **Status quo vs intervention**
  C. **Argue?**
    1. **Not possible**
      a. **Current structure**
    2. **Free market**
      a. **Principles exploit**
    3. **Environment**
      a. **A resource**
      b. **state intervention**
II. **Where economy and environment meet**
  A. **Bali**
    1. **Obstacles**
    2. **Gov't vs econ**
  B. **Econ soln**
    1. **market/technol**

Diagram created in Inspiration ®
by Inspiration Software ®, Inc.

Information audit

OK – now it is time to get serious. By now you should have your:

▶ **word count** breakdown
▶ **analysis of the question, learning outcomes, academic criteria**
▶ **first thoughts**: colour-coded themes, questions and crossings out.

Gather these together; now we need to do an information audit to identify what information we will need to find out (research).

Use a grid (see below) to write down any themes you can identify from your first thoughts out and fill in the information as fully as you can. This will produce a guideline of what you know (and what you don't). It may also highlight areas that will be hard to find evidence for, so you can seriously consider whether or not to include these.

Theme	Keywords	Evidence for	Evidence against	Example

This will be useful for **planning the paragraphs** of your essay later on as it will provide all the information you need for the **paragraph plan** (see p. 35).

Gathering information

In professional courses such as healthcare, business and education there are usually two aspects.

Firstly you will recognise that you are expected to produce *evidence of your reading and studying*. This research is the '**theory**' of your subject and includes the concepts, models and ideas of the key players in your field.

The **second** aspect is the **practical application** of this knowledge. Usually you will be asked to examine a scenario and link the 'theory' you have learnt to your professional practice.

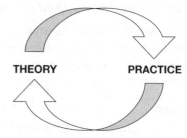

Other courses do this slightly differently as they require the application of knowledge (theory) to inform understanding (practice).

For example, in History of Art the theory you learn will inform how you see or understand a painting in practice. All courses have these components.

This is what your tutor will want you to demonstrate in your essay.

Look back at your information audit and adjust it with this in mind.

How reliable is your evidence?

Where are you going to get the information you need? You will need to refer to **reliable sources** such as *textbooks*, *journal articles*, *published statistics*, *official publications* and *publications from professional bodies and organisations*. These sources will have been peer-reviewed by professionals – that is, they have been read and checked by others working in the same research area and are regarded as reliable.

Sources such as *Wikipedia* and *some websites* are **not regarded as reliable**, as you cannot always check who wrote the information or whether it is accurate or not. It has not been peer-reviewed so its reliability is in question. Use Wikipedia to find initial information, but then move on to more reliable sources to use and reference these. Newspapers and radio programmes may alert you to issues you can follow up, or provide illustrations of a trend or viewpoint. They are not, however, reliable evidence of 'fact' or high-quality research. For this you need the genuine research itself.

Use AABBCC to check this out – especially when evaluating web pages:

Accuracy   Authority   Bias   Breadth/depth   Currency   Compare

Adapted from Howe (2001)

Check your sources now – it's as simple as AABBCC

Accuracy: Check the accuracy of the information you find. Can you find the same information elsewhere? Did the author reference it? Does it 'fit in' with what you already know? If it 'feels' wrong, it probably is.

Authority: It is best if the author of your source is a well-known expert or organisation; then you can be sure they know what they are talking about. Check the website pages to establish who wrote it and if they wrote any printed material you can find.

Bias: Is the author trying to sell something – a product or a viewpoint? Check who wrote it. A drug company will not be negative about their product, will they? But a research organisation might be.

Breadth/depth: Is the information detailed enough? Is evidence provided to back it up? You may need to fill in any missing gaps from other sources.

Currency: Is the information up to date? If not, can you find more recent sources? Tutors like journal articles because they are up to date. Web pages are especially hard to find dates for – check the properties or 'page info' option but beware; being up to date is no guarantee of accuracy.

Compare: Compare your information with other sources; this will help you have confidence in it. It will also have the benefit of showing you a range of views – useful for your essay – and extra sources for your reference list.

Adapted from Howe (2001).

Sources checklist

Note: you need to be able to **tick** the **shaded boxes**.

	Yes	No
Accuracy: Can you find the same information elsewhere? Did the author reference it? Does it 'fit' with what you already know?	Yes	No
Authority: Is the author an expert or a respected organisation? View web pages to find who wrote it – can you find anything else they wrote in a respected publication?	Yes	No
Bias: Is the author trying to sell something – a product or a viewpoint? (You need the answer to be 'No' here.)	Yes	No
Breadth/depth: Is the information detailed enough? Is evidence provided to back it up?	Yes	No
Currency: Is the information up to date?	Yes	No
Compare: Can you compare your information with other sources?	Yes	No

WE THINK....

OLD SOURCES

Adapted from Howe (2001).

Academic style

You will be asked to use academic style, so what does this mean?

Be formal

Don't write as you speak, **avoid slang** and **common phrases**, e.g. '… it went pear-shaped'. Instead say: '… it started to go wrong' or '… it developed problems'.

Use the **full version of words**: 'have not' instead of 'haven't'.

Always **explain abbreviations** the first time you use them: '… the National Institute for Clinical Health and Excellence (NICE) recommends …'

Try to avoid sexist language: chairperson not chairman.

Be remote   **Avoid** overusing *I*, *we* or *you* for **personal opinions**: 'I think that …' 'We believe that …' 'You feel that …'

This is not useful in an academic essay where you need to back up what you are arguing with evidence from the literature. You can use 'I' (the first person) when analysing or commenting on the evidence, perhaps to say how your view differs.

The exception to this is in reflective writing where it is usually acceptable to use 'I' or 'my'. Check your guidelines.

Don't ask your reader questions; they want answers. This writing style is better suited to journalism.

Be concise   Long-winded explanations usually end up being descriptive. Focus just on the point you are trying to make. Short sentences are OK. Avoid long sentences – if your reader has to backtrack it will just irritate them. Most academic sentences are about 15–20 words long.

Give definitions for technical or unusual terms unless your reader is expected to know them. Consider who your audience is.

Don't generalise – for example, 'many people'. The following sentence appeared in a student essay: *Economy has played a big part in human existence.* This earned the tutor comment, 'This is excellent waffle!'

Avoid vague terms like *nice*, *get* or *thing*.

Be cautious   Say something **may** or **could** happen, *not* that it **will** (unless you can prove it, of course): 'This suggests …' or 'This indicates …'

Researchers are usually tentative when reporting their findings because research rarely proves something absolutely. So it is better to say that the research *shows*, *suggests* or *indicates* rather than it *proved* something.

Using 'signal' words

Using 'signal' words in your essay signposts your reader through the different sections and gives them a constant stream of clues to follow. If you leave these clues out your reader may struggle to follow your train of thought. They may get confused and won't reward you with the marks your work really deserves.

Smooth things over by using words that signal clearly what you are doing.

Signal words explained

Signal word(s)	Purpose	Alternative words
Firstly, secondly, thirdly …	Show order of points made	in addition, next, then, to start/begin with, initially, additionally, lastly, moreover, subsequently, finally, previously
and …	Adding extra points	also, and, in addition, then, again, furthermore, with regard to
for example …	Introducing examples	for instance, in other words, including, the following, these include, that is, this demonstrates, such as, to illustrate this, namely
another view	Show other views/opinions	in contrast, although, on the other hand, yet, alternatively, but, on the contrary, despite, conversely, whereas, even so, otherwise, however
as a result …	Show the results or effect of something	therefore, as a result, so, thus, due to, consequently, because of this, it can be seen, the evidence shows, hence, this suggests, the implication is, one result is, as, inevitably

More signal words explained

Signal word(s)	Purpose	Alternative words
emphasise	To stress a point	obviously, definitely, undeniably, inevitably, generally, admittedly, especially, clearly, importantly, in fact, indeed, in particular
exceptions	To show exceptions	however, in spite of, yet, nevertheless
equally	To show similarity	similarly, likewise, as well as, correspondingly, in the same way, also, just as
to compare	To compare with something else	just like, same as, similar to, not only … but also, compared to/with
another cause	To show cause(s)	due to, because, another …, since, first, second
to conclude	To sum up points so far	In conclusion, to conclude, to sum up, to summarise, so, overall, consequently, as discussed, as has been shown

> **TOP TIP** Take **care with** *however*. It can be useful to signal a change of direction in your argument, but it is overused by students.

Making it flow – use signposts

Many students cram their essays with facts and references but fail to explain the relevance of these. If you do this you are making your tutor do the job of trying to work out where you are going with your argument. Make your essay easy to read by using a few simple tricks to lead your tutor gently to your conclusion and you will be rewarded with those vital extra marks. As a bonus you may even need to do less research overall.

Simple tricks to make your essay flow

1 Use signposting through the essay.
2 Use paragraphs (see paragraph plan, p. 35 and essay diamond, p. 29).
3 Use signal words to 'signpost' your essay (see p. 91).
4 Outline your essay structure clearly in the introduction (see p. 42).
5 Make sure your conclusion 'mirrors' your introduction (see p. 49).
6 Refer to the title in the last sentence of the essay.

Problem solving

Too long: over word or page count

Resolve to work to your word count next time (see p. 20). Time was wasted on researching and writing and now more time is needed to chop your work back, so double trouble. But for now look for and mark where:

- information is **repeated**; choose the best example and cut the rest out. This is hard to do as by now you love it, but just do it!
- more than one example is given – will one do? (Yes, usually!)
- **part** of your essay **does not seem to fit in**. If it does not argue towards your conclusion it may be irrelevant (unless it is a counter-argument you are dismissing). Consider cutting it out.
- you have gone **off track** or into too much detail. Are you 'waffling' and not developing your point? Check the paragraph plan (see p. 35).
- you have **quoted**. If you quote, have you also commented on what you think is important or special about the quote? A quote can't stand by itself. Use paraphrasing and summarising – this uses fewer words and because they are your own words it shows your understanding.

Too short: under word or page count

▸ **Analyse your question** (p. 23), recheck any information and learning outcomes. Is there anything you need to develop further?

▸ Check that **every paragraph** follows the **paragraph plan** (p. 35).

▸ Ensure you have a strong **introduction** and **conclusion**. These are vital for your reader to understand your work (p. 38).

Always proofread your work

Read the following tutor's comment on a student essay. After you finish laughing, remember this is from a real student essay.

> *Tutor comment*: '… note the difference between phatic and phallic … might lead to embarrassment!'

You may not have made an embarrassing error in your essay but you will have made errors that you found hard to spot.

Try:

- Reading your work out loud. Use text-to-voice software like textHELP if you have access to it. This is especially useful for dyslexic students.
- Ask someone with good English to read it. They do not have to be a subject specialist; if you have written it well they will understand it.

> **TOP TIP** Leave your work for a few days and then read it through. This allows your memory of it to die back so you read what you actually wrote, not what you thought you wrote. A good reason to finish early!

And finally: check and **double-check** your **references**.

References, bibliographies and appendices

Referencing: why are you being asked to reference?

Referencing **shows your tutor** you:
- have research skills, and can find and use information
- have read around the subject
- can provide evidence for the point you are making from your research
- can follow the referencing method used for your subject.

Why are academics so keen on referencing?

If you have taken a long time researching an area or doing an expensive study then you will want it **acknowledged as your work**. This idea of 'owning an idea or concept' can be difficult to grasp at first, especially for students from cultures where information is regarded as 'commonly owned'. As a rule you do not have to reference knowledge that is generally known in your field, or by everyone (the Earth is round, for example). You do have to reference other people's ideas. Ask yourself, 'Would I have known this without reading it?' **If in doubt reference it**.

How to reference

There are **two aspects** to referencing; you **must do both** of these:

1 Put a **citation** in the **text** of your work – this is the **in-text reference**.
2 Provide a **full reference** somewhere – at the end of your essay for Harvard and numeric; other referencing systems vary so double-check this.

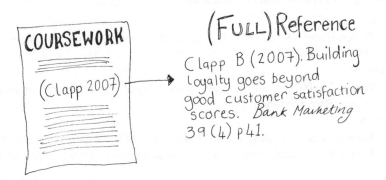

COURSEWORK

(Clapp 2007)

(FULL) Reference
Clapp B (2007). Building loyalty goes beyond good customer satisfaction scores. *Bank Marketing* 39 (4) p41.

1 Example of Harvard in-text reference

Cohen and Kennedy (2007) stated … then in your own words what their idea was.
or

Their idea in your own words followed by the reference **(Cohen and Kennedy 2007)**.

2 Example of Harvard full references

Book

Cohen R and Kennedy P (2007). *Global Sociology* (2nd edition). Basingstoke: Palgrave Macmillan.

Journal

Clapp B (2007). Building loyalty goes beyond good customer satisfaction scores. *Bank Marketing.* 39 (4), p41.

Online

Bournemouth University (2006). *Reflective Writing*. Available at: http://www.bournemouth.ac.uk/study_support/reflective_writing.html [Accessed 30/06/08]

What is the difference between references and bibliography?

References: Your list of references must contain *all* the **in-text references** (or **citations**) you have used **in the text of your work**.

Bibliography: May include books, articles and various sources you have read but not referred to in your work. It has to be very clear, however, which sources you used and which you did not. In this case you should **divide the Bibliography** into *References* (cited in your text) and *Other sources consulted*.

And finally – a note on plagiarism

All universities are concerned about plagiarism: this is where you copy information or use an idea without acknowledging where it came from.

Always keep a careful record in your notes of where you found information and include the page number in your draft versions. You only need to use the page number in your final draft if you quote directly but it will help you if you need to recheck anything. Remember, it is far better to put the idea into your own words by paraphrasing as this clearly demonstrates your understanding.

For more on referencing see *Referencing and Understanding Plagiarism* in this series.

Appendices

Information essential to understanding your point should be in the main body of the essay. Only put something in an appendix that your reader may find useful; this should be specifically referred to in your text.

Appendices may include:

- supporting evidence
- field notes
- raw or processed data (summary should be in your main body text)
- questionnaires (results go in the main body of your text)
- detailed descriptions – research methods, for example
- technical figures, tables or descriptions
- maps.

(Adapted from University of New England 2004)

Appendices should be arranged in the order they are referred to in the text. You can use numbers or letters. In your text simply put: '…(see Appendix 1)…'. Put each appendix on a new page and remember to add them to a contents list if you have one. Page numbers just continue on from the main work. Provide a contents list at the start of your appendices if you have a lot of them. The appendix goes after the references.

Note: *Appendices are not included in your word count, but this does not mean you should use them as a way to extend your word limit.*

Only include things you have referred to in your work.

12 Using feedback

You should receive feedback on your essay. Use this to improve your work in future. If you compare the comments you have received for different essays it is almost certain you will be able to spot a pattern of your strengths and any concerns.

Look at the following feedback comments on students' work. What are the most common problems?

Tutors' comments:

'So what does this tell us about the question?'

'You need to expand and justify your position.'

'Over 2 pages of description before we get to the question …'

'Lacks explanation and lapses into description.'

'Line of argument could have been tighter and more focused – set out your argument at the beginning and keep reminding us where you have got to.'

'Some sources quite old now.'

'What do *you* think? In end not sure what you think …'

'Need to criticise the models …'

'Some referencing issues …'

Using feedback to make an action plan

Try to look back at (or remember) some of your own feedback now. The same old comments are likely to keep happening unless you try to change how you do things.

Which comments or problems above most closely matched your own? Jot them down now in an **action plan** like the one below.

| I need to improve ... | the flow of my essay | I can do this by: | using signal words (see p. 91) |
| | conclusions | | using the conclusions checklist (see p. 55) |

Resolve to 'action' your action plan for your next essay and see your grades improve. Use the following table of common problems and possible solutions for ideas guidance.

The most common errors

Problem	Solution	See
Not answering the question	Analyse the question and make sure you keep referring back to it during the essay. Take special note of instruction or process words in the title.	**p. 23** **p. 25**
No structure/ Lack of organisation	Make sure you understand what is expected in the introduction and conclusion and revise the paragraph plan to organise the main body. Review the essay diamond to check you understand essay structure. Then check the drafting and redrafting section to improve the flow of your essay by using signposting and signal words.	**pp. 38–55** **p. 32** **p. 91**
Academic style	Familiarise yourself with academic style and use it. These are easy marks to get.	**p. 88**
Lack of evidence and critical skills	Avoid description. You must select appropriate evidence for your points with a model, theory or concept. Use a range of reliable sources. Provide examples if needed. Show the relevance of your evidence and example(s).	**p. 84** **p. 85**
Referencing inaccurate	Know the system you should use and really learn it – these are easy marks to get. Always acknowledge your sources.	**pp. 100**

Problem	Solution	See
Referencing: over-quoting	Review why it is best not to do this and learn to paraphrase effectively.	**p. 101**
Referencing: reliability of sources	Use AABBCC to check this.	**p. 87**
Lack of student voice	Make your position clear in the introduction. Make a comment about what you think of the evidence or any implications at the end of paragraphs. Your position must be also be clear in your conclusion.	**p. 43** **p. 35** **p. 49**

Essay-writing checklist

To finish off, let's return to Norton's (1990) essay-writing criteria (see p. 5), which show exactly what tutors want to see in student essays. This has been slightly changed so that you can use it as an essay-writing checklist.

Check you have ...

Criteria	Tutors' ranking	Have you done this?	See
answered the question	1	Yes/no	**p. 23**
shown understanding	2		**p. 6**
given an argument	3		**p. 57**
provided relevant information	4		
provided a structure with clear organisation of ideas	5		**p. 28** **p. 56**
provided evaluation(s) or your own view	=6		**p. 35**
followed academic style and presented your work as asked	=6		**p. 88**
demonstrated wide reading	8		**p. 85**
checked your English and spelling is correct (proofread your work)	9		**p. 97**
shown content/knowledge	not ranked		

Adapted from Norton (1990).

References

Bournemouth University (2006). *Reflective Writing*. Available at: http://www.bournemouth.ac.uk/study_support/reflective_writing.html (Accessed 30/06/08)

Elander J, Harrington K, Norton L, Robinson H and Reddy P (2006). Complex Skills and academic writing: a review of evidence about the types of learning required to meet core assessment criteria. *Assessment and Evaluation in Higher Education*, 31 (1): 71–90. Available at: http://www.aston.ac.uk/downloads/lhs/peelea/Elander2006.pdf (Accessed 30/06/2008)

Gibbs G (1988). *Learning by Doing: A Guide to Teaching and Learning Methods*. Oxford Further Education Unit, Oxford Polytechnic.

Howe W (2001). *Evaluating quality*. Available at: http://www.walthowe.com/navnet/quality.html (Accessed 30/06/2008)

Norton L S (1990). Essay writing: what really counts? *Higher Education*, 20 (4): 411–42.

Price G and Maier P (2007). *Effective Study Skills*. Harlow: Pearson Education.

RMIT (2006). *The Reflective Cycle.* Available at: http://www.dlsweb.rmit.edu.au/lsu/content/2_AssessmentTasks/assess_tuts/reflective%20journal_LL/cycle.html (Accessed 5/05/2008)

SCORE (2006). *Graphic Organisers.* Available at: http://www.sdcoe.k12.ca.us/score/
actbank/sorganiz.htm (Accessed 3/07/2008)

University of New England (2004). *Appendices.* Available at:
http://www.une.edu.au/tlc/aso/students/factsheets/appendices.pdf (Accessed
25/03/2008)

University of Southampton (2004). *Planning and writing your essay – an overview.*
Available at: http://www.soton.ac.uk/studentsupport/ldc/docs/Essays%20text%20
2004.doc (Accessed 1/06/2008)

Williams K (1995). *Writing Essays.* Oxford: Oxford Centre for Staff Development.

Useful sources

Cottrell, S (2008). *The Study Skills Handbook* (3rd Edition). Basingstoke: Palgrave
Macmillan.

Index

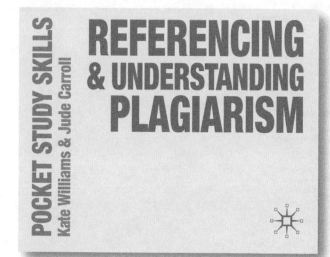

POCKET STUDY SKILLS

Kate Williams & Jude Carroll

REFERENCING
& UNDERSTANDING
PLAGIARISM

POCKET STUDY SKILLS
Julia Copus

BRILLIANT
WRITING
TIPS FOR
STUDENTS

POCKET STUDY SKILLS

Kate Williams

GETTING CRITICAL

POCKET STUDY SKILLS

Andy Pulman

BLOGS
WIKIS
PODCASTS
& MORE

POCKET STUDY SKILLS
Sue Robbins

SCIENCE
STUDY
SKILLS